A TRUE BOOK™

United Arab Emirates

ANTONIA D. BRYAN

D1361182

Children's Press®
An Imprint of Scholastic Inc.
New York Toronto London Auckland Sydney
Mexico City New Delhi Hong Kong
Danbury, Connecticut

Library of Congress Cataloging-in-Publication Data

Bryan, Antonia D., 1946 –
  The United Arab Emirates / by Antonia D. Bryan.
      p. cm. — (A true book)
  Includes index.
  ISBN-13: 978-0-531-16888-2 (lib. bdg.)   978-0-531-21361-2 (pbk.)
  ISBN-10: 0-531-16888-3 (lib. bdg.)   0-531-21361-7 (pbk.)

  1. United Arab Emirates—Juvenile literature. I. Title. II. Series.

  DS247.T8B79 2009
  953.57—dc22   2008014792

Produced by Weldon Owen Education Inc.

2 3 4 5 6 7 8 9 10 R 18 17 16 15 14 13 12 11

Find the Truth!

Everything you are about to read is true *except* for one of the sentences on this page.

Which one is **TRUE**?

T or F   Most people living in the United Arab Emirates come from another country.

T or F   Bustards, jirds, and dhows are all animals found in the United Arab Emirates.

Find the answers in this book.

3

Contents

THE BIG TRUTH!

Skiing in the Desert

Camels have two sets of eyelashes to protect them from dust and sand. ➡

The city of Dubai started as a small trading settlement on the Dubai Creek. Today Dubai is the most populated city in the United Arab Emirates. Traditional-style boats still ferry people across the river.

CHAPTER 1

Miracle in the Desert

Just 60 years ago, this country had no electricity, no telephones, and no public schools. People rode on camels, not in cars. But today, it is one of the richest nations in the world. It boasts skyscrapers, superhighways, and excellent free education. Welcome to the United Arab **Emirates** (UAE).

More than 80 percent of the UAE's population live in cities.

Land of Sand

The United Arab Emirates is a little smaller than the state of Maine. It is located on the eastern edge of the Arabian **Peninsula,** along the Arabian Gulf (Persian Gulf). The UAE is part of a group of countries known as the Middle East.

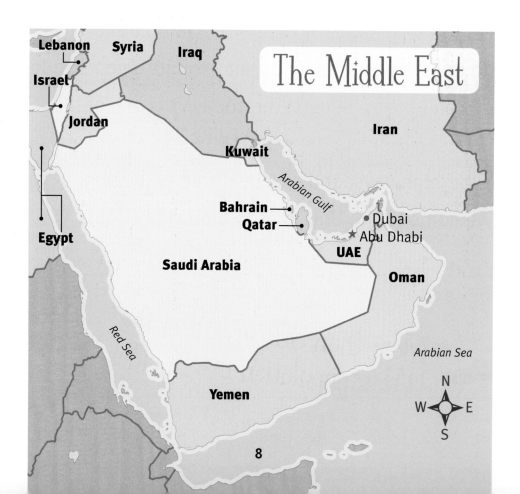

The Middle East

Lebanon · Syria · Iraq · Israel · Jordan · Iran · Kuwait · Arabian Gulf · Bahrain · Qatar · Dubai · Abu Dhabi · UAE · Egypt · Saudi Arabia · Oman · Red Sea · Arabian Sea · Yemen

N · W · E · S

Rainfall in the UAE is usually less than 5 inches (13 centimeters) a year.

Beyond the river known as Dubai Creek lie miles and miles of desert. Some wild grasses can survive in the dry sand.

The UAE is not an easy place to survive. More than 70 percent of the land is desert. Beneath isolated **oases**, however, there is underground water. Along the coastal lowlands are many miles of salt flats, too salty to support life. There are rugged mountains in the northeast.

A Lucky Strike

The UAE's rapid development began after vast amounts of oil and natural gas were discovered in the 1960s. The country's wealth has quickly turned undeveloped villages into modern cities. Today, the UAE **exports** its oil and natural gas all over the world.

Some of the UAE's wealth has been used to protect its natural resources. Hunting and overgrazing have caused some native animals and plants to become endangered. But now the government has established nature preserves to help endangered species survive.

Species that were once hunted in the UAE, such as the oryx, are now protected.

Sure Is Hot!

The climate of the UAE is extreme. Summer temperatures climb to more than 120 °F (48 °C). Desert sand can get hot enough to burn bare feet badly. On a hot desert day, a person needs about 18 cups (about 4 liters) of liquid to survive. Not every species needs that much water, however. Jirds are small desert rodents. They can survive without drinking. They get their water from the seeds, fruits, and other foods they eat.

Jirds are one of the few animals that can survive in the deserts of the UAE.

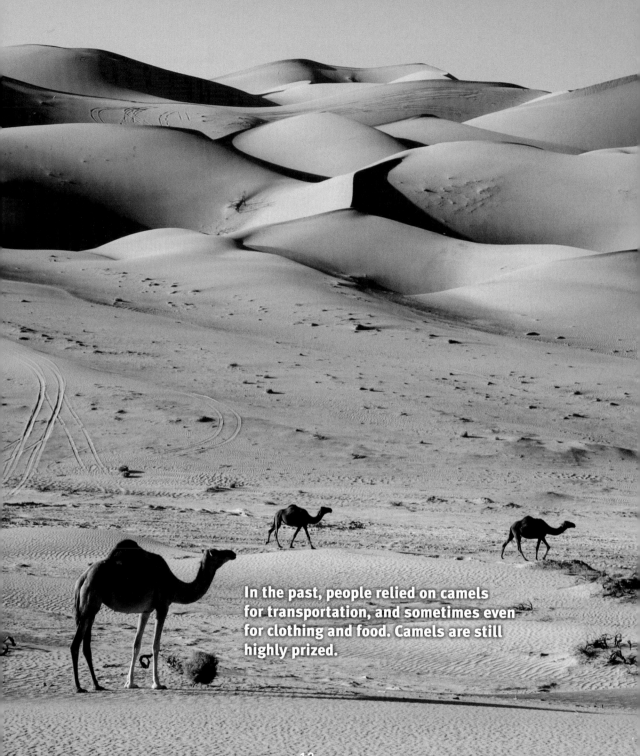

In the past, people relied on camels for transportation, and sometimes even for clothing and food. Camels are still highly prized.

CHAPTER 2

A Nation Forms

Dhow sailboats are still being built the way they were centuries ago. ➡️

For many centuries, the area that is now the UAE was populated largely by **nomads**. They herded camels and grew dates. People near the coast fished and dived for oysters that held precious pearls. Extended families formed tribes with fierce loyalties. Those loyalties are still important today.

The Tribe Has Spoken

Before the UAE was formed, the British had a lot of influence in the region. They selected tribal leaders to rule individual emirates. The British maintained treaties that tied them to the emirates until 1971.

After becoming independent from Britain, seven of the emirates formed a **federation**. This was the United Arab Emirates. The capital is the city of Abu Dhabi, located inside the emirate with the same name. Each emirate has its own ruler, called an emir or a sheikh (SHAYK).

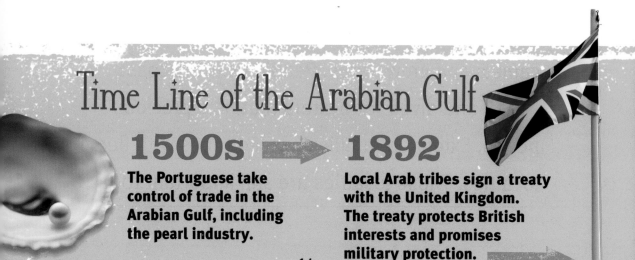

Time Line of the Arabian Gulf

1500s ➡ 1892

1500s
The Portuguese take control of trade in the Arabian Gulf, including the pearl industry.

1892
Local Arab tribes sign a treaty with the United Kingdom. The treaty protects British interests and promises military protection.

The seven ruling sheikhs make up the Supreme **Council** of Rulers. They run the country and choose the president. Each emirate also has its own local government to deal with regional issues. Sheikhs hold open councils, or meetings. There, tribesmen can bring concerns directly to their rulers.

Citizens of the UAE rarely vote. However, there is a **parliament**, called the Federal National Council. Some of the members are elected by UAE citizens, who gained this limited voting right in 2006.

1962 ➡️

The first oil is exported from Abu Dhabi.

December 2, 1971

The British end their relationship with the emirates. The federation of the United Arab Emirates is established.

Make It Work

Nomadic life in the desert is disappearing. Since the oil boom, new industries have provided more jobs in the cities. There are more jobs than there are citizens. Thousands of workers from other countries come to the UAE to build buildings and ships, work in hotels, and do other jobs. Eight out of every ten **residents** are foreigners. Most are men from poorer parts of Asia.

Dubai is constantly undergoing new construction. At times, 25 percent of all the world's cranes are being used in Dubai.

One Dubai hotel, called the Jumeirah Beach Hotel, was built in the shape of a breaking wave.

Today, citizens of the UAE, called Emiratis, are more likely to work in offices than outdoors. There are many opportunities for business people, scientists, teachers, and students. Universities have been established. Tourists flock to the new hotels and luxury resorts. The country is fast becoming the most popular vacation spot in the Arab world.

The Sharjah Heritage Festival takes place every year in the Sharjah Emirate. Musicians play *laywah* music on an instrument called the *surnay*.

CHAPTER 3

Dance and Design

Desert cultures in the UAE excelled in arts that were practical and portable, made with simple materials. People made baskets, mats, and even boats from date palm **fronds**. Women wove cloth with richly colored patterns. Today, many people still practice the most portable arts of all—poetry, music, and dance.

Some European woodwind instruments are based on the Middle Eastern surnay.

These dancers celebrate Eid ul Fitr, the most important festival in the Muslim year. It marks the end of the holy month of Ramadan.

Rhythm Sticks

Traditional dances are still performed on special occasions, such as weddings. One favorite dance recalls ancient battles. The men make bold, war-like movements to the beat of drums and tambourines. Once, they danced with swords and guns. Today, they use sticks instead.

Humble Homes

In the past, people lived in simple structures. Nomads pitched long, low tents on their desert journeys. In oases, people built small houses from dried mud. Roofs were made with palm tree leaves. Forts and **mosques** were built from stone and mud brick. A few of these stone buildings still survive today.

Some traditional Arab houses feature wind towers. They help to circulate breezes through the buildings to keep the insides cool.

Tomorrow's Towers

In the gleaming new cities of the UAE, architects are designing buildings unlike any others. Some of the new architecture will house great art. Two of the most famous museums in the world are planning extensions in Abu Dhabi. One is France's Louvre. The other is New York City's Guggenheim Museum.

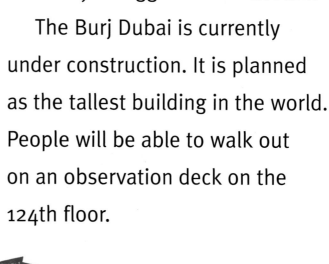

The Burj Dubai is currently under construction. It is planned as the tallest building in the world. People will be able to walk out on an observation deck on the 124th floor.

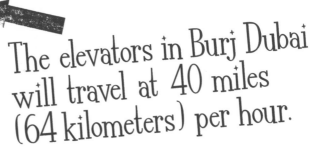

The elevators in Burj Dubai will travel at 40 miles (64 kilometers) per hour.

The Burj Al Arab hotel in Dubai was designed to look like the sail of a traditional Arab sailboat. It stands 1,053 feet (321 meters) tall.

Take Your Pick!

At Ski Dubai, visitors have a choice of five ski runs. Winter clothing, ski boots, skis, and snowboards are supplied. Chairlifts carry skiers up the mountain. There is also a place for children to play in the snow.

On Top of the Shops

Ski Dubai is on top of the world's third largest mall. It covers a space of 243,000 square feet (22,500 square meters). That's about the same size as three football fields!

Skiing in the Desert

In Dubai, the temperature is often in the high 90s. Where there once was sand, engineers have built a 25-story, snow-covered mountain with ski slopes. Ski Dubai is the world's biggest indoor ski park!

The Jumeirah Mosque in Dubai was built in 1978. However, its decorated dome is typical of ancient Islamic architecture.

CHAPTER 4

Society Rules

Islam has been the UAE region's official religion for close to 1,500 years. Today, 96 percent of UAE citizens are Muslim. Five times every day, observant Muslims take a few minutes to pray. Islam was first taught in the 600s by a **prophet** called Muhammad.

Traditional mosques have domes and tall, thin towers called minarets.

Muslims stop to pray at work, at school, or even by the roadside.

During prayer, Muslims face in the direction of their holiest city, Mecca, in Saudi Arabia. Some Muslims gather to pray in mosques. Others stop for prayer wherever they may be. Prayers are in Arabic.

With so many foreigners, the UAE is tolerant of other religions as well. These include Buddhism, Hinduism, and Christianity. At Christmastime, you'll even find Santa Clauses in some of the enormous shopping malls.

Lots of Languages

Arabic is the official language of the UAE. But many other languages are spoken, too. On the streets, you may hear people speaking Hindi, Urdu, or Persian. English is widely spoken. It is commonly used for business communication. Emirati children start learning English in kindergarten.

The Arabic alphabet has 28 letters. The language is read from right to left.

NO CAMELS & HORSES

قف
STOP

In the big cities, signs are in Arabic and English.

Sheikh Zayed, former president of the UAE, wore traditional robes and sandals.

Outward Appearance

Some Emirati men wear business suits. Many wear traditional long, white robes. White robes help reflect the sun's heat. On their heads, men wear small caps under flowing headdresses. Children may wear Western dress, but not shorts or short sleeves. Tourists are expected to dress modestly, too.

It is part of the Islamic faith for women to cover their heads and necks. Many Emirati women wear long, dark robes. Some cover their faces with veils, showing only their eyes. Other women choose to wear modest Western clothes instead.

The robes Emirati women wear are called abaya. This style of dress dates back centuries.

For special occasions, such as feast days and public holidays, Emirati girls dress up in traditional clothes.

CHAPTER 5

Family and Friends

From kindergarten through college, education is free for UAE citizens.

In the UAE, families tend to stay close. It is common for children to grow up in a home with three generations of relatives. Uncles and aunts often live nearby as well. Like many Arab cultures, the UAE has a long tradition of welcoming guests warmly. In the past, when people struggled to survive in a harsh desert environment, being welcomed with food and drink was important.

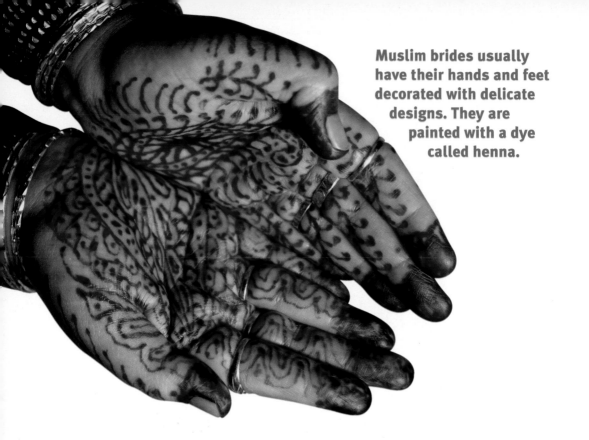

Muslim brides usually have their hands and feet decorated with delicate designs. They are painted with a dye called henna.

Traditional Women

Weddings are a favorite reason for families to celebrate. Traditionally, the bride is not seen for 40 days before the ceremony, except by her family members. Singing and dancing start a week before the wedding. Men and women celebrate separately.

Modern Women

Emirati men are expected to support their families. They are responsible for handling business affairs outside the home. Women do all the household tasks. Women's roles are changing, however. Today, at the United Arab Emirates University, there are more women students than men. Many women become teachers. They also do other important jobs, including military and police work.

The first female police patrol in the UAE was established in 1999.

POLICE

Traditionally, Muslims do not use knives and forks. They eat using only their right hands.

Holy Food

Breakfast in the UAE often consists of dates, yogurt, and coffee. Lunch is the main meal of the day. Families sit on the floor around a cloth with plates of food on it. In the evenings, people usually eat a light meal.

For Muslims, the holy month of Ramadan is a special time for worship. Everyone except the very young, old, or sick **fasts** each day from sunrise to sunset. At the end of the day, the fast is broken with a meal and prayer. Then people visit their family and friends. Ramadan ends with a three-day celebration.

Dates have been grown in the Middle East since about 4000 B.C.E.

During Ramadan, Muslims at the Al-Safa Mosque in Dubai break their fast with a meal after sunset.

Trainers, called falconers, work very closely with their falcons. They train them by rewarding them with food.

CHAPTER 6

Sporting Life

Alongside modern sports such as soccer and cricket, traditional sports are still very much alive in the UAE. **Falconry** has been practiced in Arab countries for many centuries. Falcons were captured and trained to hunt other animals to feed the owner's family. When food was scarce in the desert, falcons helped people survive. Today, men enjoy falconry as a sport.

Some falcons dive at speeds of more than 120 mi (190 km) per hour.

The Return of the Dhow

Once, pearl divers sailed through the Arabian Gulf in wooden boats called dhows. Today, Emiratis race dhows along the same routes. Dhows are easy to recognize. Each one has a high stern, a single mast, and a triangular sail. Craftsmen build dhows by hand using knowledge passed on from generation to generation.

Dhow races were introduced by the UAE government to maintain the ancient knowledge of dhow making and sailing.

Go, Camel, Go!

Camel racing is a popular desert sport. The camels used to be ridden by young children. But this practice has now been banned in many areas. Today, the jockeys are robots! The robot controllers drive around the racetracks in four-wheel-drive vehicles. They lean out the windows with their remote controls. The drivers do their best not to hit each other!

Preparing for the Future

Some of the "sports" in the UAE serve its booming tourist industry. The UAE has built huge theme parks, water parks, indoor ski slopes, and other tourist attractions. Beaches and desert safaris also attract millions of tourists each year. Dubai now makes more money from tourism than from oil. The country is also establishing industries, such as shipbuilding, aviation, and electronics. New industries and technology are mixing with ancient faith and customs in this vibrant, modern country. ★

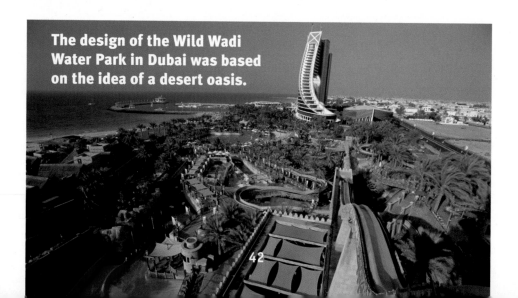

The design of the Wild Wadi Water Park in Dubai was based on the idea of a desert oasis.

True Statistics

The seven emirates: Abu Dhabi, Dubai, Sharjah, Ajman, Umm al-Quwain, Ras al-Khaimah, Fujairah

Land area: 32,300 sq. mi. (83,600 sq. km.)

Population: About 4,620,000

Percentage of Emirati nationals: 20

Percentage of land able to grow crops: About 0.8

Barrels of oil produced per day: 2.5 million

Currency: Dirham (1 US $ = 3.67 dirhams)

Number of TV Stations: More than 40

Number of date palms: More than 40 million

Did you find the truth?

T Most people living in the United Arab Emirates come from another country.

F Bustards, jirds, and dhows are all animals found in the United Arab Emirates.

Resources

Books

King, David. *United Arab Emirates.* New York: Marshall Cavendish, Benchmark, 2008.

Miller, Debra A. *United Arab Emirates.* San Diego: Lucent Books, 2004.

Mitchell, Stephen. *Genies, Meanies, and Magic Rings: Three Tales From the Arabian Nights.* New York: Walker Books for Young Readers, 2007.

Sonneborn, Liz. *United Arab Emirates (Enchantment of the World).* New York: Children's Press, 2008.

Stone, Caroline. *Islam* (DK Eyewitness Books). New York: DK Children, 2005.

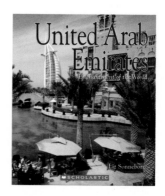

Organizations and Web Sites

All About Emirates

www.emirates.org
Visit here for some facts and figures, a time line, and places of interest in the UAE.

UAE Archaeology

http://uaeinteract.com/history/e_muse/em_strt.asp
Learn about the UAE's ancient history in this virtual museum.

Places to Visit

Arab American National Museum

13624 Michigan Avenue
Dearborn, MI 48126
(313) 582 2266
www.arabamericanmuseum.org
Learn about the traditional Arab world and Arab people in the United States. View Arab art and photographs.

International Museum of Muslim Cultures

Mississippi Arts Center
201 East Pascagoula Street
Jackson, MS 39201
(601) 960 0440
www.muslimmuseum.org
The museum celebrates the contributions Muslims have made to the world.

Important Words

council – a group of people elected to make laws or rules

emirate (EM-uh-rit) – a state run by an *emir*, or a prince

export – to send goods to another country to be sold there

falconry – the sport of hunting with falcons, hawks, or other birds of prey

fast – to go for a long time without eating

federation (fed-uh-RAY-shuhn) – a union of states, nations, or other groups joined together by agreement

frond – a large leaf that divides into parts called leaflets

mosque (MOSK) – a building used by Muslims for worship

nomad – a person who moves from place to place

oasis – an area in the desert where there is water

parliament – the group of people who have been elected to help make the laws and govern a country

peninsula – land that juts into the sea from the mainland

prophet – a person who seems to know certain spiritual or religious truths

resident – someone who lives in a particular place

Index

About the Author

Antonia D. Bryan's favorite courses at Harvard University were in creative writing, and she has been a writer ever since. She loves making up poems and has written three children's books and many museum audio tours for children filled with funny voices and wacky sound effects. She lives in New York City with her almost grown-up son and her enormous black and white cat, Sylvester. Now that she's discovered the United Arab Emirates, she'd love to take a trip there.